Lemons into Lemonade

Poems by

Pamela Martin

Lemons into Lemonade
Copyright 2009 by Pamela Gowan

All rights reserved under International and Pan-American copyright conventions. No part of this book may be reproduced, stored in a retrieval system or transmitted in any form, electronic, mechanical, or by any other means, without written permission of the author.

International Standard Book Number: 978-0-578-02383-0

Illustrated by Kathleen Hardy.

Table of Contents

Part I

Island Hoping	9
Weeping Willow	9
"Born Again"	9
Publish and Perish	10
Coffee, Tea or Me?	10
"Holy Rowers"	10
Macular Degeneration	11
Whipped Cream	12
Abstraction	12
Forward, ho!	12
"High on Life"	13
A Mobile Home	14
Post Haste!	14
Effervescence	14
Letter Perfect	15
Cacophony!	16
The Chicken or the Egg?	16
E pluribus unum	16
Fair Warning	17
An Uncharitable Donation	18
A Knee-Jerk Reaction	18
"Return the Favor"	18
"The Cha Cha"	19
A Stroke of Genius	20
A Psychotic Break	20
Creationism 101	20
"Re-Parenting"	21
Only You	21
The fall from Grace	21
Allah mode	22
"Nothing but the Truth"	22
Bail Outs or Hand Outs?	22
D.C.S.	23
The Final Touch Down	23
Depression Hurts	23
"Kitty Lit"	24

Part II

W.M.D.	27
Dead in our Tracks	27
"They Only Come Out At Night"	27
The Challenge	28
Not an Ounce of Prevention	28
Flunking Out	28
Xenophobia?	29
Campaign Rhetoric: 1968: "Jobs, Oil, Taxes"	30
Campaign Rhetoric: 1988: "Taxes, Oil, Jobs"	30
Campaign Rhetoric: 2008: "Jobs, Oil, Taxes"	30
Long Live Rasputin!	31
Diogenes of Sinope	33
"!"	32
"An Unchained Melody"	32
Surveillance Cameras?	33
"Run with Your Heart"	34
"Live!"	34
L'Indifference	34
Lemons into Lemonade	35
V-J Day	36
Positive Reinforcement	36
"Toilet Trump"	36
Monkey Business	37
Copyright Infringement	38
Malfeasance	38
Charles de Gaulle	38
I do mean "Maybe"	39
Warts and All	39
Photo-duplication	39
P.H.D.	40
Miscegenation	40
Patient Pam	40
Waste Not	41
Democratic Prerogatives	41
Rich Man, Poor Man	41
Au naturel	42
P.M.S.	42
Cuddly Cats?	42
Robert Albert Martin	43

Part III

Theology 101: "Medina's Temple" 47
Theology 101: "Jesus was a Jew: The Historical Christ" 47
Theology 101; "The catholic Catholic Church" 47
Theology 101: "The Light at the End of the Tunnel" 47
"My Last Best Hope" 48
Ethnocentrism or "Long-Nosed Barbarians" 48
"All Men" 48
Botticelli's Babe 49
Ignorance is Not Bliss 50
The Back Door 50
A Total Blackout 50
Indoor Cats 51
The Dawn of Time 52
Insensibility 52
"Police the Police" 52
Redistricting 101 53
Eternity in their Eyes 54
Rocking the Cradle 54
"That Creeping Disease" 54
Hackneyed 55
A Life Sentence 56
Cardiac Arrest 56
Persona non grata 56
Risk Assessment 57
Hypothermia 58
Gastronomes 58
In Perpetuity 58
October Harvest 59
In absentia 59
Ignorance of Ignorance 59
"The Friendly Feline" 60
"Joie de vivre" 60
Self-Possession 60
Dear Diary 61
"Members Only" 61
Domestic Tranquility 61
My Resignation 62
A Niece or a Nephew? 62
An Insulting Remark 62
"Well-versed" 63

Part I

Island Hoping

If I live another day,
It will be a holiday.
I will plan a getaway
To the V. I.*
When I get there I will go
Directly to the rodeo
Where I'll meet my Romeo
Who lives nearby.

*i.e. the Virgin Islands.

Weeping Willow

I have roamed this planet
For many, many years.
And I have cried
Many, many tears.
Tears of sorrow
Tears of pain
And tears of joy
I can't explain.

"Born Again"

I have passed the token test*
But does it really matter?
I keep getting older
And I keep getting fatter.
My time here is fleeting
On planet Earth.
But I'm always ready
For a "rebirth."

*A "token test" is a test to gauge language skills.

Publish and Perish

He calls it, "Golden Antelope."
I call it, "Caribou Moose."
We must convey
A formal truce.
Does it really matter?
What's in a name?
Whatever you call it,
No one's to blame.

Coffee, Tea or Me?

Waiting is the thing
I simply cannot do.
You get my motor running
And then you want to
Have a cup of coffee
Or a cup of tea.
When will you ever
Have time for me?

"Holy Rowers"

There are twenty-seven churches
On so-called "holy row."
"The God of the Living Spirit"
Is one you should know.
When you are discouraged
And haven't got a clue,
The God of the living spirit
Will come to comfort you.

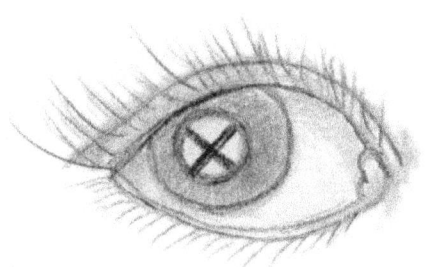

Macular Degeneration

In my periphery,
Out of the corner of my eye
I obliquely see
The world passing me by.
Kvetching is not the answer.
Complain all you will.
But, even at this angle,
I see you still.

Whipped Cream

Sweetness is the allure
You cultivate.
When I'm in a hurry,
You make me wait.
Yet you're the one
I simply adore.
And I keep coming
Back for more.

Abstraction

The parietal, occipital
And temporal lobes
Are filled with synapses
And tiny microbes.
But it is the frontal
That gives us center.
It is our teacher
And tormentor.

Forward, ho!

Now is the time
To take a chance.
Do away with chivalry
And romance.
There's no other way
I can say it.
Direction works best
When you play it.

"High on Life"

"It's my way or the highway."
You chose crystal meth.
But methadone can easily
Take your final breath.
So, let's do it my way.
Then you will see
What constitutes
True ecstasy.

A Mobile Home

If I have a car,
I can't be homeless.
Home is the place
Where I lay my headdress.
Most homes have roofs
And fire places.
I have them both
But only in traces.

Post Haste!

If you can't take it with you,
Where does it go?
To your greedy relatives
Or your favorite beau?
Either leave it
To the family
Or spend it
With celerity.

Effervescence

Soda me.
Soda you.
I think of you
When I am blue.
You make me
So very happy
Even when
I'm feeling crappy.

Letter Perfect

I work hard
At what I do.
Try it sometime.
You would, too.
I often say
It is better
To do some things
By the letter.

Cacophony!

Your music overpowers me
With its thunderous blast.
I can't take it any longer.
How long will it last?
Cease or you'll be sorry,
Sorry you were born.
Find another venue.
Your welcome is outworn.

The Chicken or the Egg?

I've enjoyed without exception
Upward mobility
And, beyond a doubt,
Sperm motility.
I had twenty children
By twenty-seven wives.
Some produced. Others didn't.
Only one survives.

*E pluribus unum**

Monotheism is a blog
We add to every day.
"There is one heavenly Father."
We must never stray.
Polytheism teaches us
There are many gods
Living on Olympus.
What are the odds?

*A Latin phrase (as engraved on the U.S. quarter), which translates "from the many one," a motto of the United States.

Fair Warning

I say to you
In God I trusted.
But I must add
I was nearly busted
For my levity
And insurrection.
I tell you this
For your own protection.

An Uncharitable Donation

You receive gratitude
And help pay the bills
When you donate anything
To the Good Will.
Give them your books
And maybe a pot
But pictures of friends
You really should not.

A Knee-Jerk Reaction

I think the kneeling bus
Is a form of genuflection
Because to kneel down
Is a true reflection
Of how you would feel
In his holy presence.
But why bend your knee at all?
To show him your reverence.

"Return the Favor"

"Pay it forward"
Is to say
Pay it back
Another way.
A time will come
When you will see
The perfect
Opportunity.

"The Cha Cha"*

One, two,
Cha-cha-cha.
Three, four,
Cha-cha-cha.
Five, six,
Cha-cha-cha.
Seven, eight,
Cha-cha-cha.

(Repeat)

*A Latin American dance of Cuban origin.

A Stroke of Genius

I stroke you.
You stroke me.
We stroke each other
So sensuously.
Stroke my ego
If you will.
I can never
Get my fill.

A Psychotic Break

When I trip,
I say, "Goodbye."
At times, I think
I want to cry.
I would like to
Take you with
But that requires
Cosmic pith.

Creationism 101

First, you write a thesis
Followed by an antithesis.
Then combine the two
To rationalize a synthesis.
Anyone can make
A basic "sillygism."
But it takes a great mind
To make an organism.

"Re-parenting"

Tabby is made of patches
And a lot of love.
Tabby is a dream.
She fits like a glove.
Sammy is a tabby
Crabbier than Tab.
We might have to send her
Back to rehab.

Only You

I am only human.
I make mistakes.
But I know for certain
My heart still aches
For that someone
I once knew
And that happens
To be you.

The fall from Grace

No means no.
And yes means yes.
Never should you
Second guess
What I mean
When I say
It's time for you
To go away.

Allah mode

Every time I turn around
I see your smiling face.
Grinning from ear to ear
Only brings disgrace.
The one thing I like more
Than a poker face
Is a visage enshrouded
In a veil of Irish lace.

"Nothing but the Truth"

Trial and error and intuition
Stand in marked opposition.
Like addition and subtraction,
They require little action.
But when you think about their worth
To those of us on planet Earth,
You would come to swear by both.
On this I take a solemn oath.

Bail Outs or Hand Outs?

We live in a casino culture.
We don't hedge our bets.
The stock market today
Is our main subject.
When it is all over
Who can we trust?
Not even Citigroup
Is too robust.

D.C.S.*

I just took a stress test
And I think I failed.
I know relaxation
Is a ship that has sailed.
When I lay down,
I arise again
Only to induce
A bad case of the bends.

*Acronym for "Decompression Sickness," which is caused by a rapid ascent, especially when diving, characterized by the buildup of nitrogenous gases in the blood.

The Final Touch Down

The "Fighting Irish" are nothing more
Than pugilistic Paddies.
When they grow up they become
Boastful sugar daddies.
When their glory days are over,
They dress to impress
Although they are the furthest thing
From worldly success.

Depression Hurts

In my mind,
I am dead.
And I say,
In my head,
I still feel
An aching dread
When I can't
Get out of bed.

"Kitty Lit"

Kitty litter is toilet paper
To the feline cat.
Without it she would have
A massive heart attack.
As if by attrition
It slowly wastes away.
And, when it does,
It's a sad and mournful day.

Part II

W.M.D.*

What we say and what we do
Diverge significantly.
But when you look more closely
What is it you see?
Anger can be little more
Than a fit of rage
Or it can be an atomic bomb,
That terrible macrophage.

*Acronym for "weapons of mass destruction."

Dead in our Tracks

If the world stopped turning,
We would melt away
Like chocolate in your mouth
On a summer's day
Or it would be as cold
As the dark side of the moon.
Either way we'd perish
Except for Brigadoon.

"They Only Come Out At Night"

We toss and turn and wiggle and squirm
In the bed at night.
When will we ever learn
This is not all right?
Somnambulism
Is a vertical dance
We can do only
In a nighttime trance.

The Challenge

There is simply nothing wrong
With too much competition.
Competition in these United States
Is a grand tradition.
Too little competition
Breeds mediocrity
That closely resembles
Incipient insanity.

Not an Ounce of Prevention

We know all too well
Everything must end.
Your mother and your father,
Even your best friend.
But we are subject to
Divine intervention.
As capricious as it is,
There is no prevention.

Flunking Out

For five and twenty years
I was an office flunky.
I think it would be better
If I had been a junky.
Then I could reside
At the local rehab center
Getting free methadone
And being a youth mentor.

Xenophobia?

Sleep not with a stranger.
He may be a thief.
And in the morning
It will cause you grief.
But how can you get to know him
Unless you try him out?
Make no bones about it,
You don't want a lout.

Campaign Rhetoric

1968: "Jobs, Oil, Taxes"

"Black-on-white crime"
Is the rage
To those who are now
Center stage.
There will be
A fall election
Without the slightest
Introspection.

1988: "Taxes, Oil, Jobs"

"White-on-black crime"
Is the rage
To those who are now
Center stage.
There will be
A fall election
Without the slightest
Introspection.

2008: "Jobs, Oil, Taxes"

"Black-on-black crime"
Is the rage
To those who are now
Center stage.
There will be
A fall election
Without the slightest
Introspection.

Long Live Rasputin!*

You must either
Smile or frown.
A frown is a smile
Upside down.
And a smile is a smile
Right-side up.
You will need
A lot of luck.

*Grigori Rasputin (1869-1916), a Russian mystic and psychic for the Romanov Dynasty (Tsar Nicholas II) during the Russian Empire, who apparently alleviated the medical sufferings of Tsarevich Alexei, the tsar's hemophiliac son. Father Rasputin was known variously (depending on your perspective) as the "mad monk," the "black monk," the "pious pilgrim," and the "faith healer" and is considered by some to have discredited the tsarist government, leading to the Russian Revolution in 1917. For a time, though, he brought "good luck" to the royal family.

Diogenes of Sinope*

If I do sound cynical,
It's because I am.
Jaded and arch critical,
I now understand
Innocence is not something
That can linger on.
It's always in the past tense.
It is now long gone.

*Diogenes (404-323 B.C.E.), the most illustrious of the ancient Greek Cynic philosophers. He introduced a wicked sense of humor into the staid philosophical canon of his time.

"!"

Writing annotations
Is a lot of work.
But I don't think
It would hurt
To know what I
Am talking about.
It might make you
Laugh and shout!

"An Unchained Melody"

I'd like to share my feelings
But I don't know how.
The words have not been spoken
At least not until now.
Many of you do fault me.
In this I, too, must fail.
But would you rather have me
Thrash about and flail?

Surveillance Cameras?

Tabby likes *eau de toilet*.
She drinks it like perfume.
But when I see her do it,
It really makes me fume.
I know I cannot stop her
Unless I put it down.
But what can I do
When I am not around?

"Run with Your Heart"

Run with your heart,
And you'll go far.
Always hitch your dreams
To a rising star.
Take everything in stride
Steady as you go
But accelerate
When that cold wind starts to blow.

"Live!"

Regis has red hair
(What is left of it).
Kelly is a "bottle blonde"
With a wicked wit.
Together they give off
A vibrant synergy.
I often wonder where
They get their energy.

L'Indifference

I love to tell the story
Of my motorcycle days.
But nobody pays attention.
They say it was a "phase."
Indeed it was daring
And dangerous to boot.
But when you think about it,
Who really gives a hoot?

Lemons into Lemonade

I can be a poet
If you only let me show it.
And surely you will know it
If I do not blow it.
But for now I sit here pondering
In the coolness of the shade
Making lemons into something
I call "lemonade."

V.J. Day

Long live the *Enola Gay!*
The war was dragging on.
Without it there could not be
A victory won.
We saved the lives
Of countless troops
But not the lives
Within its loops.

Positive Reinforcement

You can't be serious.
It really doesn't matter
If it is gossip
Or if it is chatter.
Either way I must
Fill up this chapter
Or endure a switch
Varnished with lacquer.

"Toilet Trump"

She steadies herself and readies herself.
She finally takes the plunge.
Then she laps it up
As if she were a sponge.
I know it is not healthy
Whatever lurks down there.
But Tabby doesn't mind.
She doesn't even care.

Monkey Business

You say it's better
To be a donkey.
I say it's better
To be a monkey.
Then you could go bananas
And eat a lotus
Or monkey around
Without notice.

Copyright Infringement

I absconded with your inheritance,
Your intellectual property.
Plagiarism is a form
Of highway robbery.
"I saw it on the internet.
It was mine to borrow.
Nothing is secure.
I'll be back tomorrow."

Malfeasance

I have violated the public trust
With my corruption and my fraud.
But I will get off easily.
Machiavelli would applaud.
Then I will be at liberty
To do it once again.
My actions are unconscionable.
This I can't defend.

Charles de Gaulle

I love French onion soup
But I don't love the French.
They invented sweet perfumes
For the aromatic mensch.
They protest everything.
Their revolution ended badly.
They were enamored with Napoleon.
You might say they loved him madly.

I do mean "Maybe"

You're my sugar daddy.
I'm your sugar baby.
If I had more money,
I would be a lady.
Maybe it'd be different
If this were not so.
But that is really something
We will never know.

Warts and All

When medicine is internal,
It can cure disease eternal
But can be infernal
When left unchecked.
I am but a minion
Who needs a second opinion
About this plantar's bunion
She's about to dissect.

Photo-duplication

The photocopier changed everything.
It made it so simple
To forge official documents
Without a single dimple.
It has become
The crook's best friend.
I think this duplicity
Will never end.

P.H.D.

This is my dissertation
Piled High and Deep.
It caused me so much agony
I could hardly sleep.
But now that it's all over
I can rest assured
Knowing my valiant efforts
Went completely unobserved.

Miscegenation

Some people love their cars.
Sadly I do not.
I hate to say my "Betsy"
Is almost forgot.
Sometimes I start the engine
To give her new life.
But she is misbegotten
Like a devoted wife.

Patient Pam

What doctor has no patients?
One I do not know.
He wouldn't be a doctor
If this much were so.
Doctor is to patient
As God is to saint.
My doctor has no patience.
That is my complaint.

Waste Not

Sammy has a hollow leg.
Tabby has one, too.
But I must feed all eight, it seems.
What's a girl to do?
They eat you out of house.
They eat you out of home.
But, God knows, what they'll eat
If they are left alone.

Democratic Prerogatives

I like "interactive" poetry.
It is so much fun.
It is gratifying
To know you have begun
To take part in the process
Of writing this verse.
Then you are complicit
And won't be averse.

Rich Man, Poor Man

If Pamela Martin
Could lend you her ear,
Tell me true,
What would you hear?
The crash of Stravinsky's
Dissonant chord
Or the sound of soft chanting
"My Sweet Lord?"

Au naturel

Venus was a cover-up
For female nudity
When sex was nothing more
Than a proclivity.
Women who were virtuous
Never would indulge.
But now it's an appetite
We eagerly divulge.

P.M.S.*

Pamela Martin is someone
You want as a friend.
She is that someone
With whom you pretend.
She is not real
But make no mistake.
Whatever she is,
She's not a fake.

*Acronym for "Pamela Martin Syndrome."

Cuddly Cats?

When I hold Samantha,
She cuddles in my arm.
When I hold poor Tabitha,
She cries out in alarm.
But neither thinks that I
Would do her any harm.
They are the sweetest things.
They are my lucky charm.

Robert Albert Martin (1929-2008)

My father was an enabler,
A facilitator of fate.
He tolerated my silliness
And never got irate
About anything
Lesser people would.
He was a simple man
Who simply understood.

Part III

Theology 101

"Medina's Temple"
It only takes one Muslim
To ruin it for the rest.
But I don't think the Muslims
Should be put to the test.
Theirs is a religion
Based on the sanctity
Of Mohammad's teachings.
I could never be.

"Jesus was a Jew: The Historical Christ"
It only takes one Jew
To ruin it for the rest.
But I don't think the Jews
Should be put to the test.
Theirs is a religion
Based on history.
I'm a *novis homo*.
I could never be.

"The catholic Catholic Church"
It only takes one Catholic
To ruin it for the rest.
But I don't think the Catholics
Should be put to the test.
Theirs is a religion
Based on mystery
Literally and figuratively.
I could never be.

"The Light at the End of the Tunnel"
It only takes one "Puritan"
To ruin it for the rest.
But I don't think the Puritans
Should be put to the test.
Theirs is a religion
Based on charity.
Emphatically and eternally,
I will always be.

"My Last Best Hope"

My kitties are so tactile.
Their coats are very sleek.
But I have to warn you
They are somewhat shy of meek.
They're descended from the lions
On that yonder slope.
Yet I think they are
My last best hope.

Ethnocentrism or "Long-Nosed Barbarians"*

We hope for the best
But take what we get.
And never do we ever
Let them forget
We are the greatest civilization
Known to mankind.
When you look
What do you find?

*Soon after the European and Asian worlds collided, the non-Europeans began referring to the Europeans as those "long-nosed barbarians."

"All Men"

Created or not,
We are unequal.
You are prequel,
And I am sequel.
Our mortal fate
Hangs on a string.
Nobody knows
What tomorrow will bring.

Botticelli's Babe*

It's hard to make progress
Running in sand.
You never know
Where you will land.
Perhaps on the clam shell
Covered with foam
That gave birth to Venus
On the soft loam.

* Sandro Botticelli (1445-1510), an early Italian Renaissance artist of the Florentine School, who painted the famous *Birth of Venus* (1485) now displayed in the Uffizi Gallery in Florence, Italy. n.b. Venus was just a "cover-up" for female nudity (cf. *"Au naturel"* on p. 42.)

Ignorance is Not Bliss

The time has come
For me to go.
But where and how
I do not know.
Why is that?
I answer this:
Ignorance cannot
Be bliss.

The Back Door

The gist of this subject
Is the essence of fame.
The few who have got it
Never complain.
The paparazzi may be
A pain in the ass
But it's easy enough
To give them a pass.

A Total Blackout

I'm staring at a blank page.
It is only white.
A little black-on-white crime
Would be out of sight.
When I look at my neighbors
My senses start to pale.
It's as if they're taking
The wind out of my sail.

Indoor Cats

My kitties are just like me.
They stay in all the time.
And like their lazy mamma,
They're eager to recline.
Hermetic and reclusive,
We huddle here alone
Sharing this cozy place
We call, "Our Happy Home."

The Dawn of Time

You never remember
What you forget.
You never forget
What you regret.
Regrets are memories
That won't go away.
But, when they do,
It's a brand new day.

Insensibility

Dastard deeds done dirty.
There's nothing you can do
Except clean up your act
With a cleansing tool.
If you don't remember
What you have to do,
Just do what you can
And then you will come to.

"Police the Police"

Some police are like people
Who prey on the poor.
Nobody stops them.
That would cause war.
But this odious behavior
Cannot be ignored
Until social justice
Again is restored.

Redistricting 101

What's good for the goose
Is good for the gander.
When you write it, it's libel.
When you say it, it's slander.
Gerry created
A huge salamander.
And that's why they call it
A "Gerrymander."*

*A word formed by the combination of the proper name, Elbridge Gerry, a former governor of Massachusetts, and "salamander," the purported shape of a redistricted electoral district his party created in 1812. First noticed by the painter Gilbert Stuart (of George Washington fame), it quickly became the noun, "a gerrymander," and a verb, "to Gerrymander." The noun signifies both the district and the representative elected from it. The verb describes the process of redistricting to the advantage, and the disadvantage, of certain voters.

Eternity in their Eyes

I always pet my pets.
That's what pets are for.
I love my little kitties.
It's they who I adore.
Sometimes I get the feeling
There is nothing more
Than loving these two kitties
Forevermore.

Rocking the Cradle

If men are women
And women are men,
We won't know
Who to befriend.
"Women and children"
We must amend.
Don't rock the boat.
It will upend.

"That Creeping Disease"

I already had
Fifteen minutes of fame.
Now I'll have
Fifteen minutes of shame.
I only have
Myself to blame
If I go
Slowly insane.

Hackneyed

I slave and toil
On poetry.
Why did this
Happen to me?
I could have been
A concertmaster.
Instead, I am
A poetaster.

A Life Sentence

Kissing butt and kissing babies
Is the American way.
A little osculation
Goes a long, long way
To getting first elected,
Then using your newfound power
To get reelected
Until the final hour.

Cardiac Arrest

It's been a while since I saw your smile.
Why did you go away?
I don't know if I can go
On another day.
You stole my heart from the very start,
You kleptomaniac.
You are deceived if you believe
I faked this heart attack.

Persona non grata

It comes and goes and ebbs and flows
Like the Prince of Tides.
I can stand most anything
But you I can't abide.
Even the abominable snowman
Is less loathsome than you.
You don't even know
Who I am talking to.

Risk Assessment

What is the danger
Of being alone
With a perfect stranger
And taking him home?
What is the folly
Of taking a chance
To find true happiness
And lasting romance?

Hypothermia

My body is a temple
I worship every day.
It won't last forever.
I'll be gone someday.
The gift is ours to borrow.
But I think I will
Return again tomorrow
If I don't catch a chill.

Gastronomes

Sammy doesn't think
I love her quite enough.
Tabby likes to play.
She likes it kind of rough.
Either one would say
I can call their bluff.
But the only thing that matters
Is their bland foodstuff.

In Perpetuity

Memories fade.
I'm getting older.
Be prepared.
I'm getting bolder.
I know we
Were meant to be
Together for
Eternity.

October Harvest

Octavius adores me.
I give new meaning to his name.
I have written many "octaves."
None are quite the same.
A simple man would tell you
They are ingenuous.
But a wise man would tell you
They are ingenious.

In absentia

You're the guilty pleasure
I can't resist.
But there is one thing
I insist:
Tell no one
About our tryst
Or you won't know
What you have missed.

Ignorance of Ignorance

When your get-up-and-go
Has got-up-and-went,
Then your heavenly soul
Is hell bent.
If you don't believe me
And say it ain't so,
Then you don't know
You don't know.

"The Friendly Feline"

I could write a book
About my precious cats
Because I know for certain
It is a given fact
It's their responsibility
To chase away the mice,
Lead a life of rectitude,
And take my sage advice.

*"Joie de vivre"**

I have a wealth of knowledge
Of those things I learned in college.
But you may have a better view
Of the things I say and do.
You know, for instance, life's too short
To frolic, play and cavort.
Yet you do it just the same.
You call it by another name.

*French, "the joy of everything, a comprehensive joy a philosophy of life, a *Weltanschauung*."

Self-Possession

Art through the ages
Is a mastery
Of all things human
And sensory.
I will not embellish
Or wax eloquent.
It is too easy
To be grandiloquent.

Dear Diary

To my friend
I write each day.
I tell her things
I would not say
Even as
An anecdote.
But it's her
I always quote.

"Members Only"

I laughed when you told me
You joined a band.
I cried when you told me
It would disband.
Joining is something
You ought to do
If you know
What's good for you.

Domestic Tranquility

Tell my mother.
Tell my father.
But I tell you
Do not bother
To come home
Late at night
Or we will have
Another fight.

My Resignation

I stand before you.
I have won
Your hearts and minds.
But no one
Knows what I am
Going through.
And there's nothing
I can do.

A Niece or a Nephew?

When babies have babies
Both babies suffer.
More often than not
You know who's the mother.
But the baby's daddy
Could be my brother
Or somebody else.
Maybe another.

An Insulting Remark

I'm a teacher.
I'm a doer.
I'm a shaker.
I'm a mover.
I'm a man
Who gets results.
You're a man
Who just consults.

"Well-versed"

It's better with cheddar
But worse with verse.
Sometimes I think
Poetry is a curse.

www.ingramcontent.com/pod-product-compliance
Lightning Source LLC
LaVergne TN
LVHW011430080426
835512LV00005B/368